Singing in the Dark

ALISON BRACKENBURY was born in Lincolnshire in 1953. She was educated at St Hugh's College, Oxford, and now lives in Gloucestershire and works in the family metal-finishing business. She has published six previous poetry collections with Carcanet, and a *Selected Poems* in 1991. Her work recently won a Cholmondeley award.

Also by Alison Brackenbury from Carcanet Press

1829
After Beethoven
Breaking Ground
Bricks and Ballads
Christmas Roses
Dreams of Power
Selected Poems

ALISON BRACKENBURY

Singing in the Dark

CARCANET

Acknowledgements

Magazines and newspapers: *Acumen, Agenda, Critical Quarterly, The Independent, The London Magazine, Other Poetry, PN Review, Poetry London, Poetry Review, Poetry Wales, Scintilla, Stand, The Reader, The Rialto, The SHOp, The Times Literary Supplement.*

Anthologies: 'December 25th, 12 noon' appeared in *Light Unlocked: Christmas Card Poems*, Enitharmon, 2005. 'Mushrooms' appeared in *Images of Women*, Second Light/Arrowhead, 2006. 'The beanfields' scent' appeared in *Poems in the Waiting Room*, Spring 2006. 'Schemes' appeared in *Poetry Daily Essentials 2007*, Sourcebooks Inc, 2007.

Internet: Osprey, Poetry Daily, Signals, Snakeskin.

'Affairs', 'High Notes', 'Night Shift' and '*Xerxes*, an opera' were broadcast on 1 July 2005, in *Bricks and Brothels*, a BBC radio feature about Cheltenham. 'Edward Thomas's daughter' was broadcast on 7 July 2006 in *Singing in the Dark: Back to Brigg Fair*. 'Last Entry' was broadcast on 14 November 2006, in *After the guns: a letter to Wilfred Owen*, all BBC Radio 3 interval features produced by Julian May. 'Provision' was read on 12 November 2006 by Genevieve Tudor in her BBC regional radio programme *Sunday Folk*.

First published in Great Britain in 2008 by
Carcanet Press Limited
Alliance House
Cross Street
Manchester M2 7AQ

A CIP catalogue record for this book is available from the British Library
ISBN 978 1 85754 914 0

The publisher acknowledges financial assistance from Arts Council England

Typeset by XL Publishing Services, Tiverton
Printed and bound in England by SRP Ltd, Exeter

Contents

Edward Thomas's daughter

Now winter prowls upon the hills
I write to her, her head so old
The war before the last war fills
Her mind. She lists her father's songs.

A man, I tell her, I admire:
Who steps as close as a lost child.
They sang, she tells me, by the fire
Wild Army songs before he died.

My fingertips once touched that world.
I saw it linger, washing boil,
The fire chill as long ashes curled.
Will Russia's gas put out our lights?

The robin brushes me at dusk.
Our good bones fail. We leave no mark.
His voice, she writes, was clear and quiet.
I hear him singing in the dark.

Prepositions

Through, in, over, out.
Who else troubles about

Such little words? Sail past,
You solid nouns, the blast

Of verbs drives you to sea.
Adjectives glide, still lovely.

But icebergs glare and face.
Why hack at frozen space

Unless I come to you,
Over, out and through?

Avoiding Japan

The tall boy, who hates flying, flies.
You have switched off your phone.
But your dreams wrap him with small limbs.
When you drive down alone

To your new room, the curtains flap
To Cardiff's unsought heat.
They dance a print of alphabet,
Black slashes, murderous, neat.

Your home town chirrups students.
You flee it. On the way
Down mobiles in the London coach
Tokyo talks all day.

No. Pain is unavoidable.
Cut thumbs, the treacherous man
Who shivers at ten thousand feet.
O fly me to Japan.

Puff

You leapt up, the computer's cat, then curled
On your own chair, before a glowing world
Of spidered text and viruses, would wait
Calmly, in paper drifts, as I worked late.
You tongued your ruff smooth, kept your grave eyes round,
Sniffed coffee, chocolate, till an end was found,
Or slept, sleek squirrel, in your feathered tail
So when I scooped you up, your long paws trailed,
Your chin lolled on my wrist, flowed warm past fear.
I do not think, in all your fourteen years,
You knew unkindness. But the tumour grew,
You blinked black lids to lamps as we walked through.
What sun or screen is now too bright for you?

Commuter

The siren wails across the bridge,
September's shadow sails the ridge,

The small blue car and you have gone
To Gloucester in the awkward sun

To your first job, demanding screens,
Choked copiers, your colleagues' screams.

The siren dips then fades away
Past mist-fumed fields, the motorway.

Once, under a striped jeep's canvas
You saw an elephant lunge at us.

As the lone motorcycle roared
The pony reared, then threw you hard.

There have been planes and swimming pools,
Bicycles swerving right from schools.

On wind, the last long note is spun,
Heart clenched for the most dangerous run
To Gloucester, in the steady sun.

High notes

Over the ridge, flooded tracks snarl with ice.
February shifts through its angles of wind,
North to the bare ash, east to the numbed hand.
Above the torn pasture, the buzzard's voice.

The buzzard is many birds. Dropped to the road
It rips the soft rabbit with eagle's hard glare.
As kite, it circles through ceilings of air.
It sleeps in the ash like a ruffled brown toad.

Its voices are many, a mewing prattle,
A languorous whistle over the wood.
Once, when the lambs tottered banks, it could
Draw from its throat a machine gun's rattle.

Now its voice has changed, though the night is bringing
The sun's red disc, the moon's white eye.
Its call swoops and breaks. Its mate hovers by.
To frozen acres the buzzard is singing.

10 p.m.

The mean and tidy suburbs
Quiver with fragile light.
The dark slopes spread to night
As a swallow preens its wings.

The oilseed rape whose fields
Thrust heady yellow froth,
Float a few late stars, pale moths
Upon the blue stalks' rustling.

You sit with your quiet friends.
The mobile jumps. It is him,
His voice rich with the Festival's din.
He misses you. Your blood sings,

Though he sways by the girl you have seen
Though the friends cry 'Forget him!', uncaring,
Though the rape will be stubble, unshining,
And the street will lie empty and mean.

By the bird table

John Rook. I had not thought of him for years.
Was it the blackcap, masterful and shrill,
Its pure dusked skull which stirred the lumbered fears?
The starlings dart. Their coats oil eyes, their beaks
Flash fine as needles. In a hot room, still
I sit with a huge man who never speaks.

Simple. Not quite like us. Not quite there.
Each Friday levered him into a car.
The blackcap's swoops of darkness haunt our air.
Who are these people ruffling in my head?
March blew its crooked wind and here they are.
They are not ghosts. Not all of them are dead.

His father ran an egg round, brought us trays.
It was, he said, something for John to do,
Though John sat huddled in the car. Some days
He shouted, they said, then he lashed out till
They played him the same record. Through and through
The unheard songs blared. He sat rapt and still.

The eggs were hot. Odd feathers fluttered down,
One pretty sister. Did she want the boy?
What did she try to do? They must have gone,
The owl, the wren. His new chair will tilt back.
He has grown deaf. Birds shout their empty joy.
His cupped hand hears the warmed egg crack.

December 25th, 12 noon

No, honestly, we are more organised than we look.
The piles of clothes are all washed.
I have fed the birds, then the cats,
Now the cats are out: catching birds,
It starts to unravel. The cream will not whip,
It mocks the whisk in white hissing waves.
The cat flies the long grass, scattering wings,
The creased pale blouses shiver and fall.
Time, I think, to drink, then wander
The flooded footpaths, to waver and call
And Christmas, and Merry, and to you all.

Three

There must have been a doorstep once
Where those three met and spoke,
His mad red curls, her jaunty scarf,
His thin wrists, long black coat.
I never knew them, never was
As young as they were when
Drunk with hope – and a little more –
They knew each other then.

One broke into a bawdy song.
She shook her head, beguiled,
Then pushed him down the rain-black steps.
Even the sad one smiled.
Rain on the shoulder, rain on lips,
Her coat warm as a hen
She lent one money, one a kiss,
They knew each other then.

What is known, in today's hard sun,
Is all too quickly said.
He drank. She lost her lovely voice.
The quiet one is dead.
The dog rose, heart-shaped in its thorns,
Shivers upon the stem
Glints perfect, shatters at my touch,
Never and always, then.

Welcome to the truth. Miss Bingley married Darcy.
Louisa skipped down steps, intact in pink.
Elizabeth grew fat. Anne Elliott took to drink.

But no, you cry. No truth. These deal with love.
They are the books we love. They must be right
To block, like hoods, the crowded glare of trains
Or read alone in bed on Christmas night.

On the visit

Blood. It is bad news, perhaps the worst.
So we flee, to an abbey gate
Where bosses flowing into leaf
Flicker and freeze into a face
With rounded eyes, a fox's teeth,
Wood man, blood man. Off we race

Towards the sea coast's tang and mist
Like children hiding for the day,
Join jumping boys, the quiet old,
Long hoots, short shrieks, the railway
Past parks and ragwort, Ferris wheels,
To sea's light, mocking, miles away.

Late for tea, still we drive on, where
The child's sand falls to bird's cries, mud.
Spiked samphire glows on miles of marsh.
The fishermen, returning, nod.
Tide ticks the dykes. The sky flows on.
Each samphire stem is flicked with blood.

Spooked

Their tender hot shadows
Will make horses start.
'It is you,' I cried to the old pony. 'You!'
To the young tawny mare. Yet they shied, would not stand.

One is dead, one alive. The streets stretch to summer.
Who walks grey, through shops' warm glass?
I raise a shocked hand.

The girls of the Pietà

They were the daughters of the street
Or its granddaughters. Money met
A hot hand; though the chime was brief
One spasm stopped thick blood's relief.
Its rhythms drowned by muscles' ache
The soundless kick, the low dress strained,
The clients cut off like a song.
The red-face bundle dumped upon
The doorstep of the Pietà,

Which, in the end, sunk to the way
Of Venice, with the girls turned whore.
But in its prime, trained voices soared
In monthly concert, ringless hands
Grasped the viola's varnished band
Musicians, oddly, called 'the soul'.
With artless hair, they stood in rows
Each starch-stiff bodice whiter than
The watery couplings of the sun
On their scrubbed floor. Their music's flood
Washed round the seated; velvet hoods,
Boots tight on strong calves. All were still.
Breath, by those sounds and stone floors, chilled.

The concert ended. Freed to night's
Warm tide, pairs walked, hands clasping light.
One, as the girls packed music sheets,
In silence sought the dark wet streets.

High walls

This is my contract with the rich:
They may keep their big gardens
With the lush deadly darkness of yew
From which a bird dives, past my shoulder. Soon
I will be yards from the hot road,
Watering my patch,
Where a frog rises, olive,
Plump as the moon.

Visitors

Hummingbird hawkmoths hover.
Tawny wings – grey bodies – blur.
Three-inch tongues whip and flutter
Valerian's rose-pink flower,
Mauve spires of buddleia.
The bees ignore them, dapper
Workers fed winter sugar,
Humped bumblebees, who stagger
To line cold clay with nectar.
Both hawkmoths speed to cover.
Cautiously, like a swimmer,
A bee begins to hover.

Provision

The horses of the First World War
Shipped out to Egypt with the drafts,
Sold, without oats or tack, were found
Starved, scabbed, in Cairo, between shafts.

A charity gave less cruel bits,
Vets, water troughs, to slake some pain.
The ribbed sides had sunk, finally,
When the troopships sailed east again

With cavalry horses, all hand-picked,
Big in bone, packed hard with oats.
A groom I knew marched through Iraq
To haul their buckets, shine their coats.

That war too ended. There they stood,
Sixteen hands high, without a spot
On their smooth shoulders. Do not say
Soldiers learn nothing. They were shot.

From the Portobello Road

Little bronze horse, the lady says
Your flouncing tail and your bold face
Cooled in Vienna, in nineteen-ten.
Black coffee voice, her shaking hands,
Her deep-hacked twitching hope could be
Child of that darkened century.
Who is that old man, frail as snow
Who rustles chips by her lamps' glow?
Amongst the cracked gold cups and fans
You tense with life beneath my hands.
If your danced, crooked legs are fake
They are as fine as love could make,
Your fetlocks sharp. My notes will go
Into this dust-rich travelling show,
Her stall, her life (who is that man
To whom she speaks so softly?). Can
I leave you here with empty packs
Of painkillers? Did she once act?
'I shared a horse then with John Mills –'
Your bronze eye glints. The money spills
To Nellie Lenson's coughs. The storm
Broods Portobello, cloyed and warm.
We laugh. We eat. We say goodbye.
In my bag's island dark, you lie.
But on my shelf's slow dust you burn
As Europe smokes, in twenty-ten.

Waking

To the mare's cream side
Stepped the fawn from the wood.
It nosed her wet grass
In the light's first flood.

The lorry driver saw,
Through the flash of sun –
Braked, ran back.
The fawn had gone.

Today's Talk: Sounds of the Universe

Meteors whistle. So does lightning.
Cape Town's flash hums London's streets.
A solemn boom sends our heads shaking.
Deep as sea, our sun's heartbeat
Grows quick and rough, blots out the streets
Out-pulses the stalled shuddered bus.
Wait five million years. Its heat
Will soar, a red giant, swallow us.

Big Bang passes, whoosh to whisper.
Saturn's dust hits probe controls.
What makes that squeaking, blackbird chorus?
I think I slid in a black hole,
Whose note, rung deeper than our ears,
Impatient of quick human music
Bubbles, every million years.

The talk is done. The beat is gone.
Lost in my life, I stray to buy
Ice-cream. The shop was taken over.
Vast boxes fill the purring fridge.
I walk on past a tangled hedge.
That is where she found the daisies

Rough and white, slipped from the garden,
Picked by the little Polish girl
Who came, with taller friends, to work
A year or two, crammed in small flats.
But she is smaller, blonder, younger,
Back from her wandering course round town;
Bites her lip – the gangmaster shouts –
A silent child, hangs her head down.

Poland. England. In the daisies
She dips her face. The scent is gone.
England. World. Soft thud. She closes
The tiny flat. The sun beats on.

6.25

My day begins with darkness
Since I get up too soon.
Hung vast above the garage end
A brilliant moon

Ignores the morning radio,
White sea without an ebb
Freezes the lithe ash twigs
A glittered web.

The light is metal, deep and pure.
It is what Plato's cave
Ached for, truth, the throb of power
His shadows gave.

It borrows from the animals
Snow of the owl's wing
Flash of the badger's white cheek, wet
From tunnelling.

Gleams slide from gutter, shed and slate,
The radio plays on.
I burn my toast. The east turns blue.
The moon has gone.

Carried away

Jeff Buckley, singer, drowned 1997

Walk, with clothes, into the river:
You could stay young and strong for ever

In all their minds, although they knew
The Mississippi tug chugged through.

The soar of voice, the race of blood
Could not stop darkness or the mud.

The plane dropped low. Your drummer spat
At clouded light, 'Death is like that.'

He watched the helicopters pound,
Beams cut, men shout, but nothing found.

'So sorry –' toned the phone to space,
The Southern police. Her name was Grace.

But still he prowls the polished floor
You loved, he had not seen before,

You could walk, whistling, through the door.

He saw the bank. It was not wide.
He knows you reached the other side.
He heard you reach the other side.

The old cat

How furiously you clean your white paws,
Soaked by the storm, in the kitchen's glow,
Which will soon be still at the garden's end
In the new moon's wash, the quiet of the snow.

Oedipus at Colonus

This time I will not sleep.
My frantic daughter jogs me on the arm
Afraid of sudden fall, noisy alarm.

How could you ever sleep
Before a king with burnt-out worlds for eyes,
Grown daughter, like a child, who slumps and cries?

Soaked, fearful, as in sleep,
I climbed the ridge. A glance from where I was
Lightning split sky to earth, a snaking flash.

Oh love, all these will sleep.
Toss down the coffee spoon, reach to a rhyme,
The night rain beats and drums us out of time,
Swept dark, the lime trees flower.
There will be time for sleep.

Night shift

In strange back lanes behind high flats, shuttered for Sunday,
                                        workshops still,
I walk from town, coffees, small talk. The clouds, enormous,
                                        bloom and chase
Above the black, three-cornered shack whose pools of light and
                                        oil spill.

For Max is working, by the sign which jokes of horseless carriages,
With Charlie's name, who skilfully rebored worn engines,
                                        year on year,
From Jaguars (gripped by anxious hands) beloved Minis, Land Rovers.

But Charlie died, as Max did once, when he was young Max.
                                        In his head
Metal plates grate. The garagemen thought his long head was
                                        not the same
Before uncombed curls rusted grey, feet, as he dragged engines,
                                        shambled.

The young Inspector in his suit reeled through our door.
                                        'It's Dickens' time
Up there. There's hardly room to squeeze, past piles of engines,
                                        boxes, tools.'
Since Charlie's death, he works alone. I glimpse the gangway, lit.
                                        The whine

Of grinders guards the open door. Unseen must be the hayloft stair.
The strip-lit office dazzles, bare, but for a calendar of lakes,
No deadlines, engine blocks, spilt oil. Its birches tremble. Max is there.

Schemes

Who plants forsythia now? It is not tasteful;
Too ragged, tall, and dull when leaves are out.
But see the sparrows rush into its heart,
Eyes stroke it, raw and golden as a shout.

Young, gifted

What could they give? 'See. He was beautiful.'
And she? Beech shadows flutter. Cool and clean,
A long face smiles, amused to be nineteen
For ever, breaking once again, all rules.
A husband's ageing voice creaks wearily.
'Remember, she would now be sixty-three.'

Quick frowns, which flowed like leaves, would etch their groove,
Dry coughs from flourished smoke-rings hack the air.
Ash would creep through the honey of her hair
Taut waist sag, from cream biscuits that he loved.
Small sins catch our teeth or tempers later.
They missed those, crashed straight into one greater.

Pills, guns or tights, pornography of death,
Remain unfondled, a brief end to grace.
What would I give you? Not to reach that place
I touched at eighteen, where the mind's warm breath
Freezes to ice. Girls, laughing, brushed past them,
Sleep left them, aching. Does the kind dark condemn?

I do, completely. They, who were so bright,
Who rode unbroken pride too far, forgot
So much in their impatience; every knot
They tore; their single loneliness, each night
Upon the tangled bed. Mind's hot, dry dance
Gave later love, time's hidden leaf, no chance.

Yet if they lived, would they now fail again?
Find, grimacing, a thin note on the mat?
A child might not have rescued them but met
Her own dark places. They scrawled words, whispered song.
Lilac unwraps from frost. Breath floods my head,
Savage, yet sweeter, because they are dead.

Six poems

After hearing the songs of Nick Drake (1948–1974)

His own hand

I must stop thinking of his death.
It crashes round my mind
It will not go.

I hurry down the garden.
My breath is smoke.
By the wet tongues of fern
I fill the water bowl.
The birds, high in the plum tree,
Wait for me to go.

Evening

Wait. I must not listen to sad music.
So I will talk to you of sun or cars,
Then stare at the high wasteland of the stars
Which whistles through our bones, as iron hums bars.

Blackbird shouts from lilac. Is this music?
Although he practises in that quiet time
When holly sharpens, green flowers drop from lime,
The small roofs loop his voices, swoop and climb.

Now I have written cheques for every bill,
Swept fine dust from the floors and windowsill,
Rich as my bankrupt country, drunk my fill.
Before each power fails, I hear sad music.

On the way down

Clearly, your hair was your glory,
As they said of women once,
Glossy, thick as a pony

It hid you like a mob.
It strayed across your shoulders.
You would not need a job.

So when you burst in anger
At useless friends, their stare
Took in first the lank and unwashed hair.

Why would you care, now? After,
Some, before slow sleep,
Drum a tune. Their fingers

Soften, without a mark.
They knead your scalp, the clean hair,
Which brushes back the dark.

He

Someone without compromise or chatter
Practises till nerves and strings are taut,
Unbrushed by the honeysuckle's pollens,
Perfects that trick of thought

Which he can master only when he hears
The clearest voices clouding in his head.
Can he bring coffee's heat, white scud of sky?
No, reader. He is dead.

Alma Road

Found, lost so quickly! I drive the dark street,
Tall as a barracks, with odd gardens, neat
Dry tideless gravel; some softer with weed
I would have rushed by. Now, I see
A clump of iris five feet high,
Yellow as kingcups, the tumbled sky
By the quick Windrush, the small hot stones
On which I leaned, at twenty-one,
Stunned this could be. Great yellow flags
Will spring each year by dustbin bags
Lively as blood. Oh do not mourn,
So quickly found, so quickly gone.

Gone

He was not easy in his body.
Let him be wind, rain's scent, ride air.
I stare at the sun's battered grass.
I cannot see him there.

Only a bird throbs, straight through heat
Without a sound.
Bullfinch? Linnet? In the quiet
The branches bound.

Wait

Barbarians shout at the gates,
Once let them through, they own the land.
My hands press hard on splintered wood.
I do not know which side I stand.

Polar

Your dream, antarctic. Down the crevasse
The husky howls at his master's face.

The snow, which flowed through the tent flap, blows
Past caked hood, chill bone, into the soul.

Your legs drag numb through unflinching white,
Too far to cross. At the drop of night

Breath on your back is the bear, who rakes
His claw through guts – But then you wake,

Pad to the January door and stare
At the mild street. It is all out there.

Mushrooms

Have you found them, before day glowers,
Their nestled domes in glistening white
From heavy dews which whispered light
Simpler than kisses? They are earth's true flowers.

Their scent is ground's breath, older than the sun,
Frills pinker than a child's nail
Not rank brown ribs laid out for sale.
Snap the stalks quickly, for the small worms come.

How many live by fields now? Of her
This rises suddenly, the cull
My father made, a lunchbox full.
I smelt black perfume drifting up the stairs,

His autumn supper, called, awake too late,
'Mushrooms —?' sank, slept, awoke to find
Her, so rarely lit and quiet, her hands
Fine earth, the mushrooms steaming on the plate.

City cruise

With the grey Thames calm and endless
With our first half century gone
Still late, we race the jetty, on
To the tilting decks, as careless

As stubborn schoolgirls we once were.
We sprawl on seats, shake maps. Behind,
Our troubled children's charm and whine
Is over, your first husband's frowns

My two stout horses, all those cats
Who sprang like small gazelles through grass.
The docks' black stakes are torn down. Glass
Glints cones and obelisks for banks

Whose towers outstrip cathedrals' height.
You saw a psychic. Your phone summons
The lawyer in his Georgian rooms
You meet for a quick drink tonight.

We see the steps where pirates drowned
Rum-soaked, chained up to dry in tides.
Slim as a fish the cormorant flies
The clean straight river, plunges down.

They hunch in tribes on rusted boats.
We marvel at their creamy young.
I swept below each bridge, when young
With someone else. Quiet fills our throat,

Uncertain pensions, the wrong past,
Our awkward breathing. Tower Bridge
Cracks open from a road to ridge.
Between its high horns speeds a mast.

The boat bumps round. Tossed by my side
You watch the swell come at us, full,
Brown, plunging, irresistible.
'Look,' you say softly, 'at the tide.'

Infested

You shake my sleep. 'Is that a rat?'
Of course it is; the lightest scritch
Of claws on wood as it gnaws through
Paper and wool like peach and dew.

You stumble down to find the cats,
Who only spend their days on rats,
Trot crossly to their bowls again.
You heave their soft weight to our bed.

I fear a nest. The cupboards spill
Boxed stamps where Tanganyika still
Exists; white letters, skin unbruised,
Dolls' cots a child scarcely used.

Cats sleep, rough silk in pools of sun.
I drag from shelves, clothes, kites. My skin
Listens. The rat, past shout or prod
Sits hunched in calm, remote as God.

The Inn for All Seasons

I will stop here for coffee:
And in its dark perfume
Halfway upon my journey
They step into the room

The one who could not love me
Smiles, slips twenty years.
My old horse whinnies, rideable,
His quick mind washed of fears.

My tabby cat, no longer thin
Races the summer wind.
And I recall each urgent thing
My long sleep left behind,

My child without her sorrows
Long grass without chill dew,
My mother's name, that shopping list,
What I must say to you.

Here is the gate, here is the chance
The calm dark rooms will give.
The bend flies up before me.
I steer away, and live.

Main line

Breath in the dark, the air brakes snort,
The great Canadian diesel flaunts
Red mooseheads on its side. The rails
Rattle and bound, the hooter wails
Flat wagons jostle from South Wales

Steel in long rods, steel in vast coils,
North with red flash and reek of oils,
From Newport where my daughter sleeps,
Rain licking past low terraced streets,
To Chinese shopfloors' midday heat.

The heaving branches sink and sigh
The lit express train sidles by.
How flimsy its gold coaches seem
With paper cups, strewn magazines.

Keeping the keys

On a kitchen nail in another land
Hangs the key to the house in Granada

To lemons as heavy as breasts
The yard where the fountain sang.

Run your hand on its fretted black teeth.
Tenderly, rub off the rust

From the scent as a window was flung,
From the child's voice, stopped in the street.

Not the key in the air,
Not the belt with the bomb
Unlock the house in Granada.

Some families expelled from Granada in the fifteenth century still keep their house keys.

Plus allowances

It is the last vice. It is coffee,
With no kick to the head, is sex,
With no heat or sad waking. Work

Calls us from dark beds to the next
Scatter of sky, where tired children,
Worn carpet are left in suspense.

It fills the head, a breaking wave.
Intent and pure, it burns out thought.
The screen is cleared. The papers shift,

The carrier's van takes all they bought.
Machined steel piles up in its tray.
Even the voices, angry, fraught

Have been brushed briefly by its wing
Are soothed and sheltered off the phone
With a rare tact you could not bring

To dirt and tangled clothes at home
Although it is the day's last gift
To weary you, to send you home.

The Bible tells, in its long breath,
How night comes, when no man may toil.
Work slows our small and greater death.

Moles

Moles, as I mentioned above,
From habits as firm as ours
Throw crumbled mounds by the dozen
Once they smell frost in the ground.

But the battered spring creaks round,
Paddocks are rich with new dock,
White violets trespass in woods.
The mole strikes out for a mate.

As the moss dries, gold on the gates
His hot hills circle my feet
Echo dark days of the mole,
Crunched worm, his ferocious love.

Breakfast show

Radio Gloucestershire has lost the news,
Entrusted to the new girl. 'Are you ready, Max?' she calls
As the jingles crumble. Then, 'Oh dear –'

Desperately, their fill-in music plays.
We longed to be the star. Instead, we are
The one who pressed the wrong switch, on our first day's trial.
Will it go better this time, ah, my dear?

1945

Does history lie? It is too smooth;
Panzers, split atoms, new jet planes.
One quiet major who fought through
Found horses, tethered in neat lines,

Mounts of the Prussian cavalry
By Italy's rubble, Austria's graves;
Bold, fast enough for men to try
Rough races in that strange free time.

Do old men lie? But my books say
The best black geldings were brought back
For Life Guards' mounts, on guard all day
By London streets, to doze and sigh.

Did German mumble through their bits?
Did oats from English clay taste sour?
Boredom saved them from the bullets,
To canter by the park's wide lime.

Night out

Brahms? Yes, the story. While he was drinking
The door was kicked open, a girl crashed in
A man on her arm, a brooch on her shawl.

The first drink drained, she turned, in a rush,
Wheedled, 'Herr Doktor, play something for us!'
It seemed, said the diarist, she knew Brahms quite well –

Flushed, Brahms bent to the untuned piano.
Notes flew in flocks, soft as doves, quick as sparrow,
While the girl swept the stranger through dance after dance.

How long would she last? A winter? A year?
Brahms had his honours, his pupils, his dear
Untouchable Clara, too heavy to dance.

Symphonies, lullabies, songs filled his days,
A whisper his nights. Give all to one glance,
Pound the dust's dark piano, whirl dance after dance.

Before an operation

Today, no one has quarrelled, no one died,
The beeches rise, taller where they were thinned.
November licks high fields long green and gold.
The buzzard drops in silence from the tree.
His outspread wingtips whisper on the wind.

Viewing

The films you listen to all sound the same,
That is, you watch them. It is me who hears,
Sweeping the landing, whistling down the stairs

As though these led into a different house:
The kitchen radio, the song's flowered bog.
The drugged detective wanders through the fog.

If he stepped in your film, at half-past ten
He would hear screaming, as the hatches burst.
A woman's voice goes soaring past the rest.

I do not ask what the disaster is.
The rockets plunge. The ship is swept off course,
Fire gallops down the passage like a horse.

The heroes scream, then, logically, they die.
Certainly, we would. But one grabs the rudder,
Cable, trapdoor – I do not watch that either.

So, are we doomed? Blinking, we meet the day
Just like the unseen hero. Toast is made.
I eat sweet jam, you, sour marmalade.

Affairs

Miss Monson came from Lincolnshire. So did I. As yet
I am not the only daughter of a wealthy baronet.
How respectful was her lawyer's smile.

Miss Monson moved to Cheltenham. So did I. But then
The cattle browsed by High Street upon common land, a fen.
Enclosure came. How broad the lawyer's smile!

My house has three small bedrooms. Miss Monson built up nine.
Her pleasure gardens ate their fields, would sink and swallow mine,
As her crisp notes were melted by his smile.

She built a towering terrace. She named an avenue.
Stairs swept, iron wrought, the new roof soared. Her debts were
                                                    mounting too.
A woman of your talents need not trouble, breathed his smile.

Miss Monson came to London. How hard, her nephew said,
She bluffed, then cried. The bank had failed. The list of fees was read.
Where was the charming lawyer with his smile?

She hid in France, she slipped back. She paid small bills, grew old.
Tanks loom like roofs by sweated troops. A man steps, sharp and cold,
The crude oils splash, the white teeth flash. We pay the lawyer's
                                                    smile.

The beanfields' scent

It is light as winds, without coldness,
Fresh waves of sea without salt,
It blows a sweet honey, uncloying,
It is happiness without fault.

Its flowers' tongues ask no taxes,
Though their purple is royal; their white
Is pressed by black so pure
That noon is burned by night.

Who buys a scent called 'Beanflowers'?
Its glossy blue of leaf
Buckles, to June's sharp showers.
Best things are free and brief.

Recovery room

To dart at people like a wren
Shrill, angry, was her manner then.
A shock to find the room so quiet,
Under the towered machines, her feet
Wrapped white, as by a final sheet.

'How bad she'll look,' my daughter said
On the warm train which smelt of bread.
The light dips low. These snorts are sharp.
My daughter leans, untidy, near.
'How angry she is! Can't you hear?'

Gas feeds these breaths, exact and false.
Her feet, untaught, could pivot, waltz.
I hear one longer, shaken breath.
From Lincoln's shrubberies and sills
Fast, furious, the first wren shrills.

On the air

I am a bat. My head is filled
With radio music, love, moths, grief.
It is hard to loop the low grass. I am freighted.
As the cat strikes, I chatter needled teeth.

Nectars

Honesty; fading daffodils;
Pink drunken fling of cherry trees,
Deadnettles' parted lips
Send me to crawl close corridors,
Curse rain and roofs, smell at the end
One clear drop at the tip

Which trembles. I stand drenched with gold
(Lily of valley, violet)
My perfumes ache; no time
To sleep, to feed or not to fly.
The garden whirls. I hum on breath
Rose, starred clematis, lime.

The snowdrops' icy peace has gone.
Primroses shout for me in March.
I must come when they call.
Ageing, I dream the winter's rest,
(Blank cyclamen, chaste hellebore).
Into the frail and empty cell
The first, free petals fall.

Levellers' Day

The Levellers came to Burford
They wanted land and votes.
They clattered down the small streets
With fresh mud on their coats.

Only one war was over.
They swept past Cromwell's men.
'We should have fought them by the stream.'
Luck does not come again.

They fell into the inn's soft beds
As dead men sink through earth.
Then Cromwell came, who did not sleep,
Who marched them to the church.

They huddled. From the pulpit
Their General told them why
They would be shipped to Ireland
And which of them must die.

Four men stood in the churchyard,
In first sharp scent of may
One screamed out like a child,
Then tried to run away.

One called the name of Liberty
Who waits, who never runs.
One lifted up his face and turned
In silence to the guns.

The last, who had grown cunning
Recanted and was spared
To babble from the pulpit
Of how the rest had erred.

Three men sprawled in a churchyard.
Now, in their name, we would
Sing sad songs, then chew soya.
The Levellers tasted blood.

But there is honour in this,
The slow song in the throat.
Three men lie in the churchyard
But we drive home to vote.

Sunday night

Now I should ring my daughter,
Lean by my husband, idle
In the small screen's blue sea. Instead
I read *The Horseman's Bible*.

The Mongol ponies cream the plain.
Napoleon's stallions sidle.
The smuggler's piebald rounds the bend
Into *The Horseman's Bible*.

It is not fair to fish all day,
Stroke perfect golf swings, rival
Great trucks on Harley Davidsons,
Or scan *The Horseman's Bible*.

The Russian mare's gold metal coat
The Morgan's mane-swept saddle
The Arab's turned, enquiring eye
Dazzle *The Horseman's Bible*.

What keeps us sane, through dark and debt,
Might not be love or travel
But stallions' names – Old Comet, Flyer –
Sung from *The Horseman's Bible*.

Epona, Celts' horse goddess, is
A name, a still-warm bridle.
The western sky glints Pegasus.
This is *The Horseman's Bible*.

What men march bridletracks to die?
What heretic burns, for libel
Of forelocks, or a foal's first sigh?
Give me *The Horseman's Bible*.

After

You know we are not lost. Nothing is lost.
The smallest crinkled petal of heartsease
Crumbles to ground. The wind that sweeps each face
Brings, wild with sun, your mother as a girl,
His vanished brothers, holds an endless place
For dogs, cats, ponies, robins that she fed.
Speak, as you must, of every fault and flight.
But never say of me that I am dead.

Coming home fast

The sun is sinking with the blood.
The rich green of December's grass
Glints blindly as the ice winds pass.
Through puddles, carved by tractor tyres,
The pony and I slip and glare
Through pack-ice, like two polar bears.

Scraper

John Clare's name for a fiddle

Clare noted down the gypsy's tune,
Not fire's white ash, the beer-blurred moon,
Loud nights spent with the gypsies.

His life dragged to its untuned end,
The London trips, new soft-voiced friends,
Women more used than gypsies.

He scarcely worked. More children came.
Carriages left. He lost his name.
How neat his music's pages,

Gavottes and sea songs, waltzes, jigs,
No clag of ploughland, reek of pigs.
Their notes flew off his pages.

How fast Clare bowed. He touched each string
Tenderly as a bird's spread wing.
His sons forsook the fiddle,

Ran the railways, left for good.
Did his wife stroke her apron smooth,
Without regret or anger

Reach down the fiddle by its dumb throat
Take, gratefully, the folded note?
He lived too long a stranger.

But the fine casing cracked with use,
Bundled across the inns, strings loose.
From his low chair, half-tipsy

He slung his silver, spent no word,
Tucked under arm, a sleeping bird,
The fiddle swung. Hedge shadows stirred
A sudden tune, unbroken, heard.
He whistled, loped, the gypsy.

Variety

Bull's Blood, Top Weight, Black Valentine,
Black Sugarsweet, Red Elephant,
Red Robin, Mrs Hutchinson's,
Empress of Russia, Cook's Delight,
Iraqui Heart-Shaped, Up to Date,
Poppet, Gladstone, Covent Garden.

Here are old beans, white-flowered in sun,
Fine-tendrilled peas, potatoes' gleam,
Onions' fat globes. I have grown none,
Lost travels dwindle to a dream.
By Red Squash, melons, Maltese Plum,
What have my nameless hours done?

Arabian nights

I think 'Baghdad'. It is not real,
The fairytales I never read,
The palace where a huge man stalks
Marbled, chilled and dead.

I read the dried fruit packet:
'Added sugar: none.
There are forty kinds of dates
In Iraq alone.'

The dry gold dates, the wet black dates,
Plump dates where stones lie deep.
The plane which sweeps the borders,
The child who cannot sleep.

Lesbia, later

Should I, first, have told you who Lesbia is?
A fierce Roman boy wrote her lovesongs; and yes,
Her true name was Clodia. We do not know
If she ever loved him, but branded a whore
In the longest oration of Cicero
Her answer was silence. For no more was heard,
No rings swelled dark water. She just disappeared.

So history loses us. No one dissolves
In a scornful phrase. Herbal lotions, black salves,
Would drag out her disease. She may have lived, tough,
With smooth skin; an old husband; forced to retire
To dank autumn villas where she drank too much
Then crunched down the gravel walks, carelessly dressed,
As mist teased her hair from dyed curls, uncaressed.

No, you still see Claudia, swiftly, from far,
Her new husband bought her the fast discreet car.
Her parties, though seasonal, are truly grand.
Sheafed lilies – her favourites – blaze white by her door.
She offers you, briefly, her slim unmarked hand.
The boy died, washed aside, her written-out past.
What thoughts skate her mind's pool? 'My lilies should last.'

Solo

How can the oboe
Sing like a woman?
The long hair flows
Down the player's back.

How can he – yes, he –
Hold breath so long?
Young planets flee
The black horizon.

Dew gleams the long slopes
Of the park.
The notes fly fast
As bees from dark.

Wrap me in sleep
Toss down this care
A tumbled tune
A glistening hair.

In orbit

Silent and huge, Mars swings close to our earth,
Astronomers write with a flourish. Breath
Will leave for space winds, before Mars comes again,

Skims our horizon, as low as a bird,
In August's calm country. Light leaves the world.
Farm gates loom in wheat. That the great planets spin

Always, invisibly, under our rain,
Noon's glare, confounds me. Blue faded, I scan
Sky's fields. 'Any luck?' owners cry. Bats' soft spin,

Their soundless anger, misses me. Moths whirr,
The pony's white flank moons through docks. I stare
At true moon's slice, their roof. Quick brightness rings

Over the tiles. 'That's it!' my dark hosts cry.
I drive out of their sphere. Sky-dazzled, I
See street lights, comets, orbit once again

Wrong roundabouts. But was that really all?
I stand in my own world, the grubby hall,
No bats or flighty stars: a nagging pain.

At one a.m. the cat and I walk out
Magnetic, straight. It rises like a shout.
Mars, vast and milky, hangs, flashes the bull's red rim.

The century is three. Our second war
Circles. The soft plants droop. The heatwaves soar.
Astronomers are wrong. Mars comes again, again.

Marking time

How many hours have I leaned on horses
In leaking stables, to wait for the rain
To end, while a glistening ear-tip flickers
The swallows criss-cross to their eaves again
While the lightning prints its electric whites
In the dark beyond sight; as on my skin

Flanks steam slow clouds of heat? Rain pounds. But birds
Foray. The woodpecker, greener than grass,
Rakes flooded ant-mounds. Magpies bound, tails flirt
Long rides of air, the highest pines' blackness,
The lorry pours sheets. Hedgesparrows creep out
Dry as the sun, dapper grey as a mouse.

The rough, cowslipped grass, which the pony mows,
Falls steeply down to a binder-twined fence
First hammered by hands which, ten years ago,
Dropped in spring from the gun, without defence,
Whose fields steam haze, whose pied cattle glow,
Where clouds roll over the owned horizon.

Two horses fell. Now my hands have worn thin
Under mud's scabs, brown grass-scuffs, scratching hay.
If I wash these lost hours off like a stain
I will find much undone, more waste, wet may
Tumbling. Green world breathes and turns, to that day

The warm mare and I ride into air with the rain.

October's

The mist is creeping down the ridge,
Down hills with strange names, Cuckoo Pens,
As watersnakes melt into fens
It drowns the copses, licks each hedge.

A mile away, in standing ponds
White washes at the pylons' feet
As boiling waters silk and meet,
Wet ferns wave spring, with glistening fronds.

Fog, only fog! But ash trees bend,
The hawthorns in the hedges run.
Sleepless as the sentry's gun
Black firs, like cat hairs, stand on end.

Bloodlines

No blood is pure. My father's page
Has Vikings' height, their blue-eyed rage.
But from my mother's house I hear
The rapid speech, a Welsh chief's name,
Her father's grandfather who came
Out of a farm in Monmouthshire.

I have crossed down to the deep West.
Wales broods an hour away. At best
I trundle termly on bad roads
Through ploughed-up orchards, Cardiff's streets,
My daughter's boxes and defeats.
The Severn glitters miles of mud.

I speak no Welsh. I cannot sing,
Yet talk in floods. I claim that lying
Ease; and how, wet year on year,
I rode Welsh Cobs. They too, cross bred,
New Forest, Arab, Thoroughbred,
Once turned for home, picked up their knees.
Their Welsh manes snapped, they ate the breeze,
Trotted full tilt down English roads,
Back to the farm in Monmouthshire.

February 14th

Snowdrops on a wet bank, in a suburban garden
Nod through red docks; as I, in a howl of wind,
Claw weeds from the soaked clay. The trains echo by
In the cutting's gleam below.

Half a century ago
(Where have those Sundays gone?) great drifts of snowdrops
Lit a wood's banks. There no one weeded them
But deep black snow of beech leaf.

Along its cratered drive,
The old house reared. A farmer thought
To keep a mistress there. He never did,
She chose new brick. He was a chill man
Who married money. There was another woman –
In some spring fit, some hope, he planted all those flowers,

Or the gardener did; but well. They spread
Down every bank, dense, pure, their scent slight honey.
I trust they are still there. I press cold clay,
Wet to glint of bulbs, quick toss of snowdrops,
To brief wind. Below me, in the cutting,
The great trains rattle lovers to their hopes.

First lights

No wonder the world is warming.
It is Sunday morning,
No one is up. Sun is streaming
Into southern rooms, sweat is silking
Breasts, the tiny curls of hair.

Half-dressed, I run out where
The shrieking blackbird cries
In trance of frost, seeds' hiss.
The bald moon drops from skies.
My bare feet, pointed north,
Clamped to your heat, are ice.

Season's greeting

Autumn sat slumped beside the motorway.
'Broken down?' she cried. 'Good. So have I.
Call this September? See that scorching sky –'

'Well done,' I soothed. 'You managed blackberries.
My favourites.' 'Do not touch them! You will choke.'
I nibbled on sour blebs . Their taste was smoke.

Autumn, I saw, was smoking like a chimney.
'Look what you have done, your Hoovers, cars,
Hair dryers, strimmers! Will some kindly star

Give you a second chance?' 'Where are the swallows?
The wires are bare.' Her lashless eyelids dulled.
'They left me early. Birds are never fooled.

Though trees blow green as April, the hot winds
Thicken with diesel fume, Sahara's dust.
You spray my apples' bloom. Your harvests rust.'

My van, an hour late, roared to a halt.
She ground down the last stub-end, vicious, neat.
Coke's scarlet, teazels' gold, flared at her feet.

Lincoln OS 121

I buy this map for my Italian friend
Who in her hand-hemmed skirts at the war's end
Lived here; longs to go back.

Her Romans built the knife-straight major road,
Not that which wandered villages, I drove.
Here are their names. Go back.

Hemswell and Harpswell, Blyborough, Patchett's Cliff –
That limestone ridge we laboured up, whose rift
Sang water under land,

The spring's thin pulse beside the thrush's stone
A scoop of yellow shell, song's bubble gone,
Out of the noon's flat land.

Vast fields were sprayed by planes. The people kept
Their kindness, but grew sad before they slept,
Lincolnshire's curse, black blood.

Though skies bloomed, they blew higher in the Fens.
The cod's salt coast lay out of sight, land's end,
Laws, votes, remote, slowed blood.

Will Elena find high lanes choked by cars
The swede field crammed with houses, strange as Mars?
Will she mourn going back?

What makes or breaks us rides us to the end:
I murmur, like the spring, each name I send,
Brigg, Riby, Horkstow Grange, my long-lost friend,
I never shall go back.

Recycling

I met the postman on the drive,
Spread letters, glued to one by rain,
In kitchen corners, dug again.

I had a catalogue of coats.
My husband had a bill or two.
Your letter was an interview.

Cooking, new boyfriend on his way,
You floated with a cream-lit spoon.
I came in dirt-streaked, planting done,

Glimpsed something pale beneath my boot
A cream card stamped with 'Tokyo',
Frail spider writing 'Sapporo

For Christmas... Minus 20 here!'
The one who tore your sense apart,
Who for nine whole months, spoiled your heart.

His name, remote as garden's rain,
Which you once held as dear as blood,
Patters the floor, with useful mud.

My Kind of Day

Day dwindles. I open the magazine,
It will wait for me at the back,
To be devoured, with the last smudge of cream
In the coffee cup. I search on:
'New Feature'. My favourite is gone.

Throw the page down! I will write it myself
(The actress green-framed in her chair)
'Breakfast is brought by our marvellous home help
Who then whisks the twins off to school.
I browse the antique shops, then cool

In our courtyard pool, his latest gift.
(We have nested here for a year!)
I fuss with my ferns, then dress for my lift
To the West End.' Goodbye to that
For the Yorkshire filming, the flat

Where she knots her head scarf, a worn Land Girl.
Reports from a different war
Flicker her phone. He was seen with a girl;
Bruce has been expelled. But she bends
To flourish soaked swedes at the lens.

As London regrets the feature is off
(They chose football listings instead)
She whistles, drives home, past the scrubbed boots' trough,
Past the slow bus, where a girl leans,
Leafs hungrily through magazines.

The welder's tale

In the Clyde shipyards then, he says,
Dozens of cats ran wild,
Stalked rust-brown rats, scrounged sandwich crusts.
He kidnapped one, to find

It would not chase the daring mice
Which plundered his two rooms
But raced his walls, with feet of soot.
He bundled it back home

The sea-soaked yards, the echoed sheds.
Uncorking tea, a man
Asked 'Where are all the cats today?'
A mile away, one van

Braked quietly. But from the shed
The cats (who brought TB)
With kittens, tricks and fleas, had fled.
The cairns of scrap stood empty.

'A mile away... How did they know?'
He smiles. He ends our chat.
I scan the empty sky. I wish
I was a Glasgow cat.

Journey's End

Remember, Lincoln Rep in sixty-eight
Had a young coltish company? From those
He flashed the winner; had a heavy nose

But wild black hair, slim wrists. Yes, at that date
Realism raged. Eggs sizzled every night.
The candles blew the dugout maps alight.

He slowed his dying, with a graceful hand
Dangled from army blankets, while each flame
Was beaten out. Later, I heard his name

Amongst the Sixth Form, heavy drinkers, tanned.
One met him in a pub (no high-priced bar)
'Went out'. He could, she yawned, play the guitar.

I yearned for him. But no, make light of this,
Coach trips, dropped contact lenses, giggling friends,
His Hamlet, fur cloak heaving at the end,

As our provincial mothers glossed the Blitz.
No corpse, failure or star, he has returned
To small streets, Malvern's hills, from the West End.

Hair waves, dull grey. The perfect cheeks are bone.
Slim fingers, oddly tanned, flutter his throat.
'Musician' adds a final programme note.

We fade. By my indifferent daughter's side
I watch him drift a spoon through scentless soup,
Flushed with fatigue, duck from the curtain's swoop,

Spring to the old, fine actor by his side,
Salute him, face a flash, a breath's beat. Wait,
Did each map die to dust below the gilt
In Lincoln Rep, in nineteen sixty-eight?

Cover

Since summer is ending,
The sunflowers they grew
To lure birds to the shooting

Thrust ragged heads to view.
Their tender centres blacken
As eyes of old dolls do.

Since their stems crowd so thickly
I tramp and flounder still
On paths the storms flood quickly

Clouds part. Torn yellows spill
Flames, France, girls' hair, wake unkempt farms,
Warm every hedge and hill.

Riding on Christmas Eve

The countryside is empty. This is Christmas
When muddy cars and jeeps sail into town
When thin hands, broad hands, jostle and take down

Tinsel, paper, turkey legs, whose Christmas
Seems centuries away as I steer through
Woods on the pony, sky electric blue.

The moss creeps up the pine trees like a robe.
Two chestnut deer bounce wide winter tails;
A squirrel rattles up with his long nails.

Even the polo ponies' sweating grooms,
The white-sleeved young man, cantering easily,
Left frozen fields for drudging, luxury.

Whisper, there is in this a smudge of Christmas:
The last sun, which burns downwards like a rose,
The snort, the owl's human cry, air's rime.
White trembled whiskers frost the pony's nose.

Across the street

I do not like him, though I like his wife,
The laughing girl; for he cut down the tree
Whose hazelnuts the squirrels ferried rashly

Over to us; whose leaves waver my grass.
His fence is bare. But in the early evening
As cat and I hack roseheads, he is working,

Thickened a little, bent above his wall.
He pats the mortar sleek. His radio
Whistles from a bucket, the last glow

Catches cracked slabs, each drab and wet front door.
Snowed petals bloom my pail. I brush them trim.
He does not – I see – wish to go in

To screens and children, though September blows
A chill of trouble on cat's tail and rose,
Wraps pail and trowel so suddenly in night.

Cobs and pens

My grandfather, a small man, once walked to a swan's nest.
Air filled with hiss.
The male rose from the water, its wings whirling.
They have the power of horses, aimed and loud,

Can bully, thieve, will swagger up a bank
To thrust a beak into a child's lunchbox.

I used to see one, past the scrum of ducks
The children fed, upon the murky lake,
White leaf to close the mind's eye, slowly turning.

There is a place where hundreds come to winter
In mild Dorset, last year's young, smudged brown.
They sleep in drifts, dry leaves swept on a shore.

Kings ate them at their feasts.
Vandals break their wings.
Swans flew once, in stiff lines, above my door.

The shell

The empires fade. Villas in Spain,
Or Chedworth, crumble. Snails remain.

They sail and sway each broken wall,
No humble, thumb-sized snails that crawl

To fell your seedlings. These are huge,
Were brought to eat, be battered, chewed.

With shells translucent as dawn's floods
They slipped into the mossy woods

Missed fire and cries. Now safe, they rock
Down stony paths, until the fox

Noses their dens. Dim cream, nut-brown,
Forty rare shells lie tossed around.

The finest, violet-veined like blood
Is salvaged from the empty wood,

Washed of all trace of slime and self
Rolls up its kingdom, one bare shelf.

Pulled up

At the gallop's end
The favourite stands
His noseblood stains
The rider's hand.

The trainer sees
The nostril's drip.
The big race lost,
The fourth Gold Cup.

One small blood vessel
Fills a lung
From his old cough,
The Irish run.

A month at grass
Till he blows clear,
Time to come back
To win next year,

Or by the hedge
Small roses wreathe
To stand stockstill
Breathe deeply, breathe.

Announcement

North never was the way to go.
The legions sobered at the snow.
One boy crawled back alive.

The coach has come from Aberdeen
Where steady men by noon's hard gleam
Dig out the sheep alive.

The young boy with the crooked smile
The girl who ran the extra mile
Pause by the Northern Line.

Live safe, live dully and live long.
The voice booms out, unshadowed, strong.
'Avoid the Northern Line.'

Drought

The beech tree stands upon its toes.
A dark V opens like a house.
What creature curls in that dry space?
Not squirrel, owl. It is too low.
From ground's mean stones these arched roots grew
A barn too draughty for a mouse.

Sight shrinks, then flickers. Here they come
As quick as beetles, enter in,
A whole small army with their drums,
Their stools and quarrels, on the run.
Wood turns to paper, ink and gum,
Love letters hidden in a tree.

The raised roots will bring down this tree,
One amongst the storm's great losses.
The squirrel runs. The armies see
Skies that burst eardrums, blacken trees,
The spy's last love, letters like leaves
With final, crooked rows of crosses.

Snapshot

Your cheeks are round,
You are a winter apple,
A doting father, rich too. Yet
I could have loved you fifty years ago,
Faithless and gaunt, abandoned to your debt.

The country road

At the foot of the hill
By the old stone school
The roads fork.
Take the Oxford road, with the ruined barn
Ruinously rebuilt, the hawks
Hung on their silence
As winds beat night.

Turn right,
This is the rambling road,
Horses browse banks in sun.
Villages crowd, one by one,
Towns glint ice-creams, Italian shoes.
But you must choose.

Or must you? See. I have a map.
There is another way,
Elkstone, Winstone, a thin red line
From you to you. The hay
Crackles to the storm's blue sheen.
I will try that road one day.

Mercombe Wood

Who set these beech trees on the ridge
Tender to sunlight, black to storms,
Whose bristled seed-cups wake my hand,
Whose long twigs trail, as green blood warms?
No name wounds the grey flash of trunks,
Not even yours. As you were rich,
Lustful for fame, to the last ditch
I refute you.
But as you left high trees to sigh
To crowd tall silver on the eye
Between storm-beaten wheat and sky
I salute you.

The rooks' parliament

Rooks are not stunted crows. They are black,
Hunch quietly on fields in plough.
I woke as a child to their raw
Kind cawing. The shooters then came
Claimed they were pests. We lifted them back,
Their eyes' light a chilling blue flame.

The marksmen were wrong. Rooks eat pests.
The blunt-headed crows in their pairs
Rip road-kills; while rooks' beaks, slim, bare,
Prod every clod in their slow crowd.
Rookeries crown rough roadside trees
With clambered sticks, thriving and loud.

A strange story hovers like birds,
That their field circlings form grave
Assemblies where wisdom is made
To rule their land well, with a caw.
We cannot. Dare they? I am glad
We do not shoot rooks any more.

Enclosed

I send you the wood
with its twist of path
the old carriage road,
time of slippery stones
of broken axles,
jolted bones.

I breathe you rough fruit
where the beech trees sail,
bunched oakleaves, torn
by the night's great gale.
In your mind, grown stiffly slow,
let this world's green tunnel flow.

Though you shake your head
as a horse flicks flies
no harm or ghost in the warmed leaf lies.
Do not linger in this wood
although west winds rise,
although rain beats hard
from your treeless skies.

Tuesday

There is a storm of blackbirds.
Each bush has one.
I go to look at Venus
Who tracks the sun,

Instead, find Smudge in orbit,
Flailing, cross,
Three inches from the fine moss
Below the blackbird's nest,

So I spend half an hour
Sun beating on my head
Weaving rough string to cat–nets
Half-drunk on windblown flowers.

The fiddling squeak of blackbirds
Fills my head like sun.
Come home to quiet: a small world's end,
The nest of blackbirds gone.

I bang to tell the neighbours
But by the darkening step
The glossy bushes rustle
A fluting yap

Young birds in subdued hunger.
The day reels on, begun
With lift and lilt of blackbirds.
Venus has crossed the sun.

Thinned out

How I would have mourned these trees,
Young, thin-skinned, as though each twig
Were my own flesh, gale from breeze.

Grey, I saw they leaned too close,
Beeches' silver died to black.
Breathe, survivors, fill sky's space.

Long trunks lie, upon their leaf.
Veined wood startles, red and warm,
Solid chairs to huddle grief.

Squirrels which I would have found
Flying, black against the clouds,
Race them, two feet off the ground.

The April foal

You hoped she would be pretty. She looks wise,
Her father's darkness smudged about her eyes.

She lies, a sack of bones. The bright clouds roll.
Why is the wind always so chill for foals?

'Those pasterns slope,' her owner says, sucks teeth.
The knobbed legs plait. She staggers towards earth.

But Minuet, her tall grey mother, spins
Out of her way, then arches, draws her in.

From Germany's reunion clear-out sale
The mare came, with milk glistening by her tail.

Anxious, she bit this foal, squealed when it fed.
Is it her first? Was the first colt born dead?

Now she is calm. Her whickers are slow silk.
She guides the foal's red mouth into her milk.

The hooves shake, small as deer's. The pasterns slope.
Wind tugs the tag of tail. We can but hope.

Constitutional

When I am troubled I begin to walk.
I leave the car a mile from the ward
Then pad the wet streets, staring hard

Through archways into yards, a burnt-out bin,
Arrive ten minutes later than I meant
Quite breathless, with your roses slightly bent.

Each day of convalescence I grow worse,
I feel the pavement singing through my feet,
The bruised and fragrant peach I will not eat.

There are the ghosts of lanes near where I live,
Dense hawthorn with the chaffinch shrill as hope.
Jays screech, wake me, almost too tired to cope.

Stay in. Grow fat. Plump pillows, make more tea.
The carpets are shampooed, the curtains pinned.
The soul walks out to darkness and the wind.

Have you heard?

The clouds fold soft and grey.
They hide the sun's white face.
More rain sweeps on its way
The hills' heat fades in haze.
Can I recall her face,
The wild girl from the farm
Who drank unclouded wine
Who tugged whole tides of harm

Two children born and wrecked
Two marriages cast by.
I watched her walk this grass
Beneath June's empty sky
Lift her last child high
In her long yellow dress
Hair loose, bare shoulders sly
Her voice one slow caress.

If heartsease eyed the wheat
I do not think she cared,
If a wing's breath from feet
A lark spun up and soared.
She boasted, plotted, flirted.
But growing grey came hard,
More drink hung sour on breath
Green bottles heaped the yard.

Liver failure? She will die.
Down wet fields she claimed to own
The roe deer flashes by,
Yellow tail a dandelion.
Lost at home, in coffee
I splash Irish Cream. I stare
As its clouds unfold as softly
As the sunlight in her hair.

Out of the box

They were all different. When you raised the lid
The first dark wave of chocolate broke, but hid
The Spanish lemons, nougat crisp as France,
The English hazel and the heady chance
That alcohol would drop into your mouth
Raw smoke of whisky, Chartreuse from the South.

Milk chocolates came from small shops, a sweet silt.
The North, the Quaker chocolate makers, built
Good houses for the men, made chocolate plain,
One dark safe sin to lure you back again.
Then subtler friends produced the slim Swiss box
With tiny shells, ripe taste of apricots.

Brief Christmas Eden? Wait. Here comes the snake,
Praline, brown bubbling hell all factories make,
Which trickles on us from a glittered waste
Of wrapping – Deluxe – Belgian – but one paste
Disguised as truffles, whorls, as blank as night
Drowns cherries, nuts, rose-bright Turkish Delight.

A tiny loss, not one to cry
While children wither, old men die,
And yet a loss, handful of scents
A bouquet clasped each year by sense.
Time to scrub celery, reflect
On nut trees felled, on orchards wrecked,
How each delight, distinct in name,
Rotted my good teeth just the same.

Last entry

We see you hurtle to an end and ask
That you, lost for a lifetime, ease our hearts.
You brood on proofs, long falling out of love
And where to push the bed when shelling starts.

Xerxes, an opera

It is utterly lovely and I am asleep.
For years I have watched them, nodding away
Through poems, percussion, the old, as the young snigger
With dark pony-tailed boys, like my daughter's lost love.
They are here today; am I the only
Middle-aged soul? And I am asleep.

I surface through the slime. You are away.
You hate opera. My daughter is unhappy.
It is the hottest June an over-heated world can give.
The chair is hard. I could be in our shabby kitchen
By the radio, with the cat's snores. But I am here,
Risen to lukewarm air. What have I said?

Nothing. Sleep is silent. The flute is silk,
The voices wander air
We cannot breathe; they are their element, birds
Who need no branches. I have no story,
No synopsis. I will see it later,
All plots, sub-plots, Romilda, Arsamenes,
Flower-sellers; an ache in Handel's head.
At the interval, I will slop weak coffee, smile
At the tight-toed ladies, in my easy shoes.
But now I have swum through; sad youth, long age,
Where sleep tugs down, down.
Here is the voice, that easy bird,
The air is cool, I am awake.
It is utterly lovely.